Each Child

Written and illustrated

L.E. Perkins

This book is dedicated to all the children and youth in the world. Each of you is precious, so be proud of who you are. I hope that you have the love and support to be your true self.

About the Author

L. E. Perkins is a school counselor in New Brunswick, Canada, who works on a mental health team that provides services for children and youth.

Each child who is born

is a gift to the Earth.

A chance to be better.

A blessing from birth.

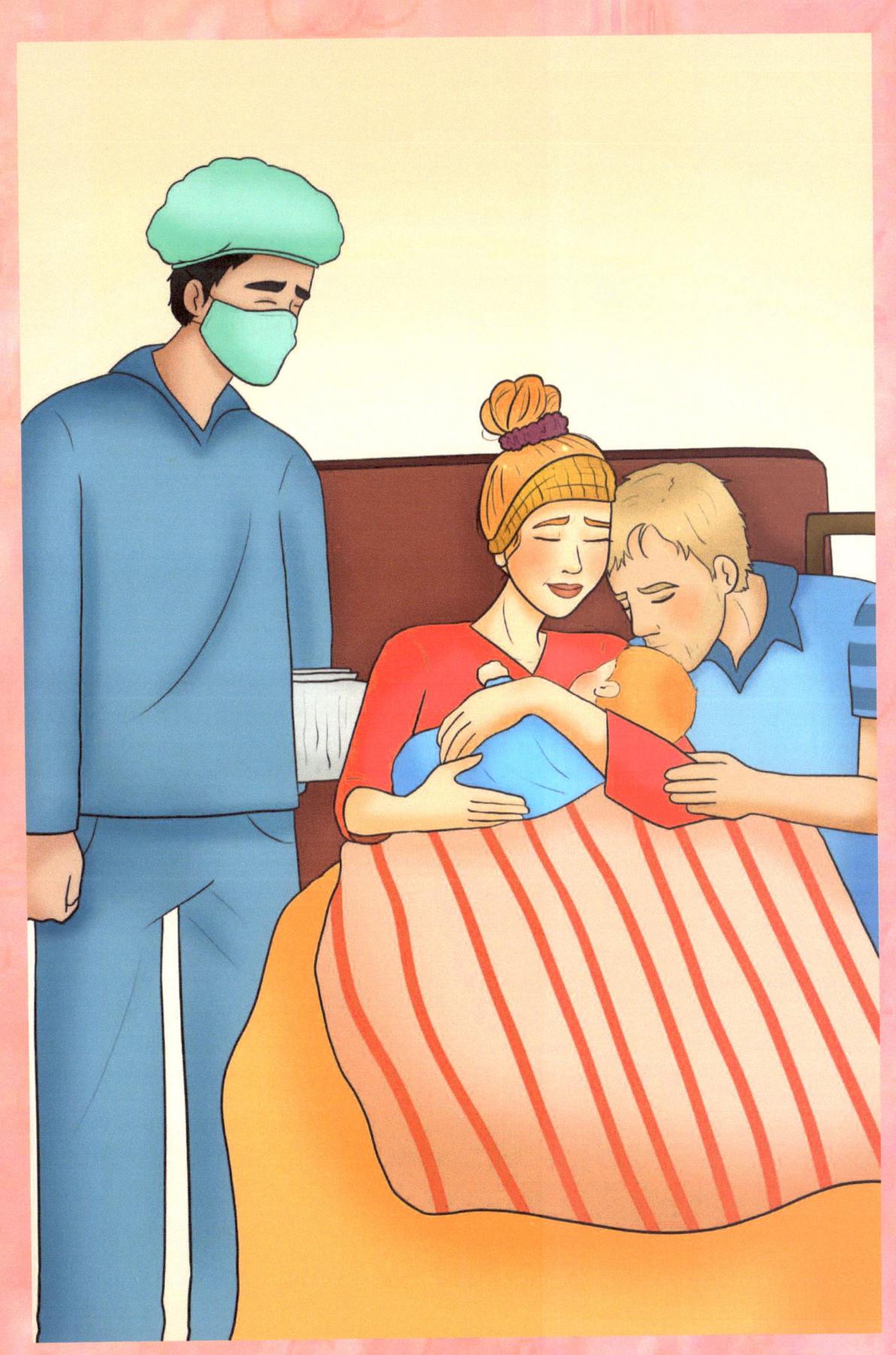

Each child is a person

Unique in themselves,

Regardless of gender,

color, or health.

Each child carries with them the gifts they will offer

and lessons they'll teach

us to make our hearts

softer.

Our job is to protect

yet allow them to grow,

Is a balance of guiding

And letting them go.

Each child will explore

to know who they are.

It's a task to support,

whether close up or far.

Each child is so precious,

A light for our course.

The person they are,

it cannot be forced.

To measure the goodness

Of those in our midst,

We just need to watch

how they treat all the kids.

Each child is a gift

So be gentle and love.

It reflects who we are

and is watched from

above.

www.ingramcontent.com/pod-product-compliance
Lightning Source LLC
Chambersburg PA
CBHW041435120626
46547CB00002B/232